A Children's Self Help Guide to Overcome Anger

Dedicated to all the children at Greenleas School, Leighton Buzzard who gave me the gift of their trust in order for me to help and support them.

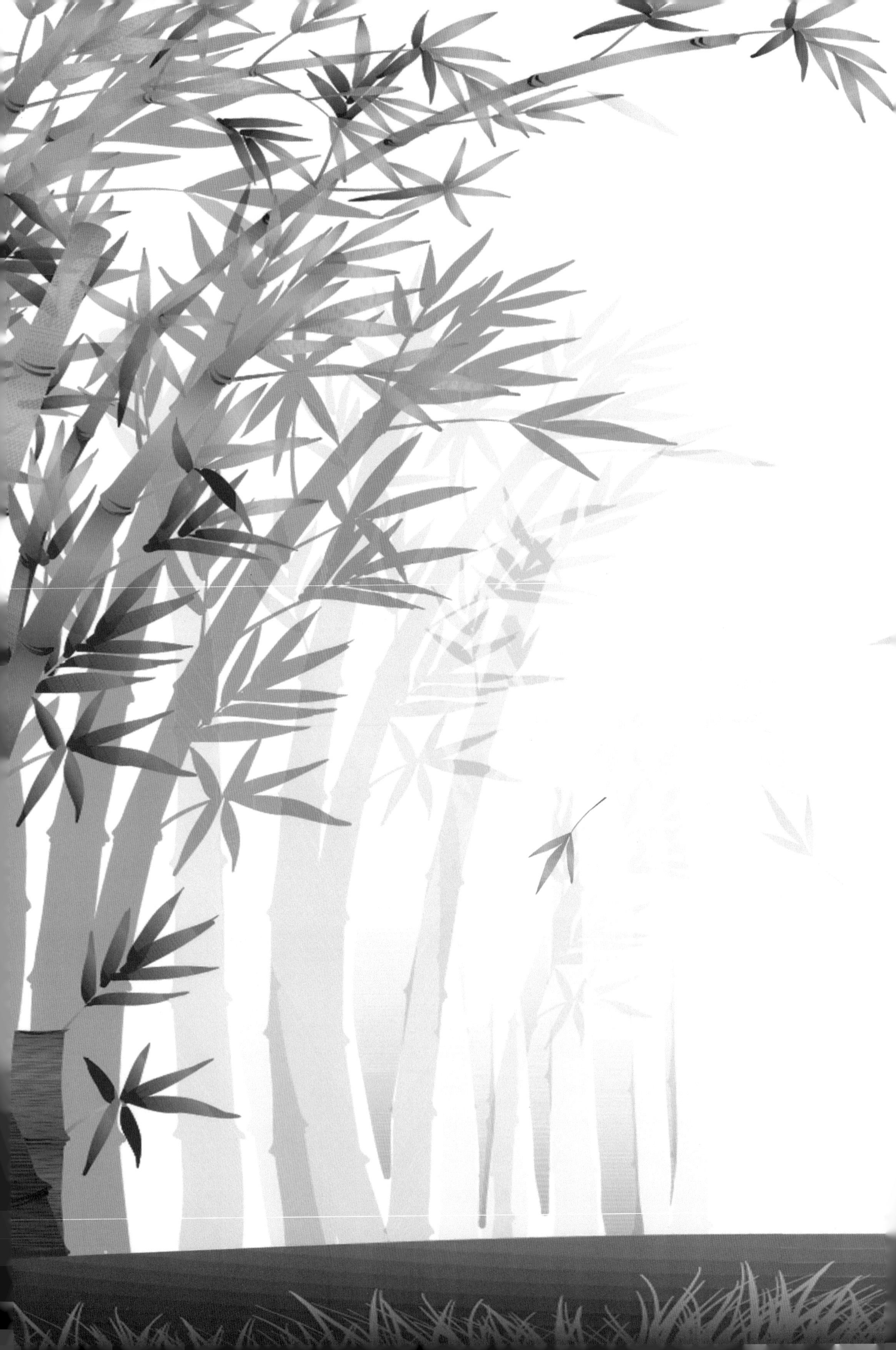

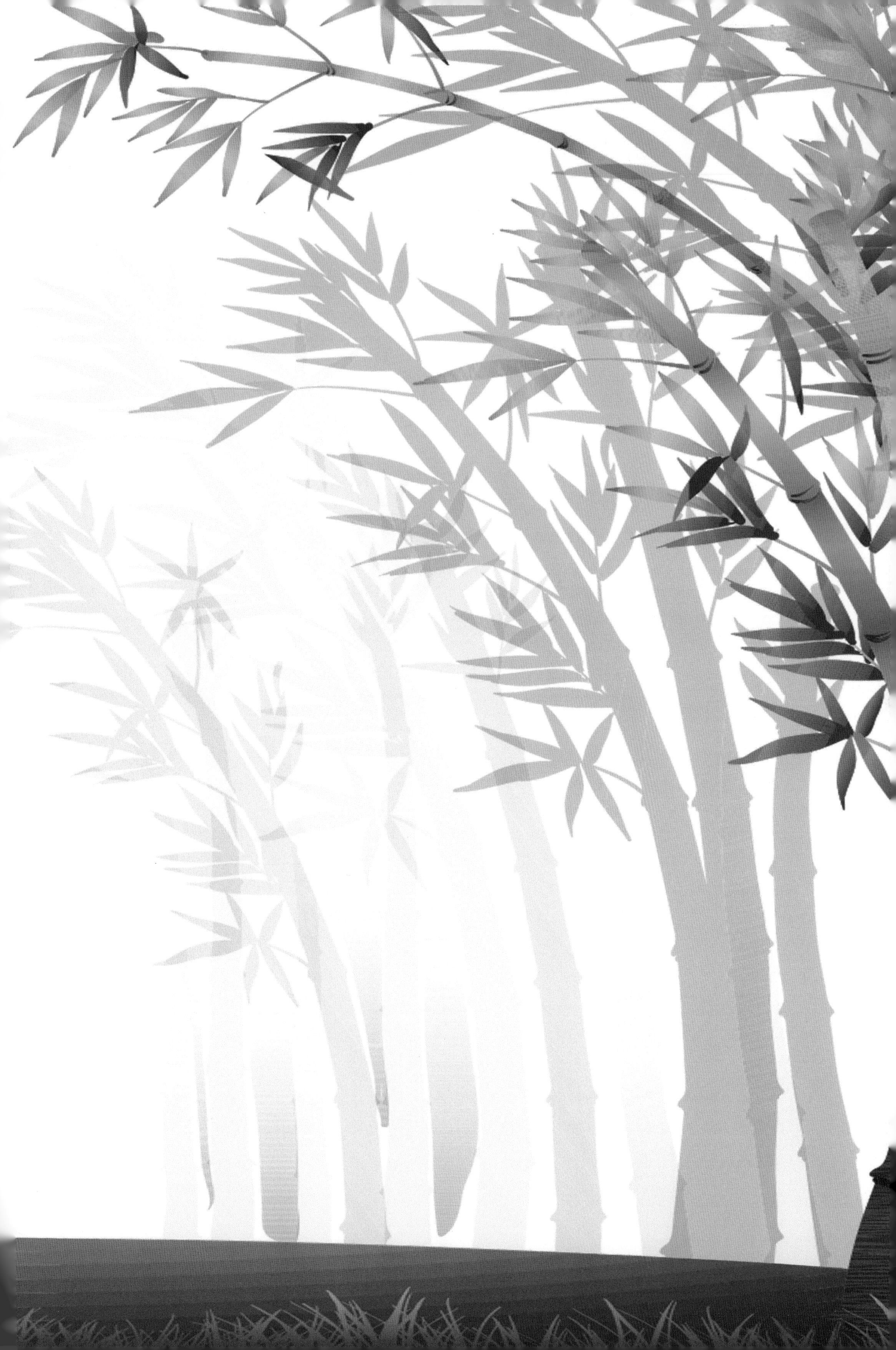

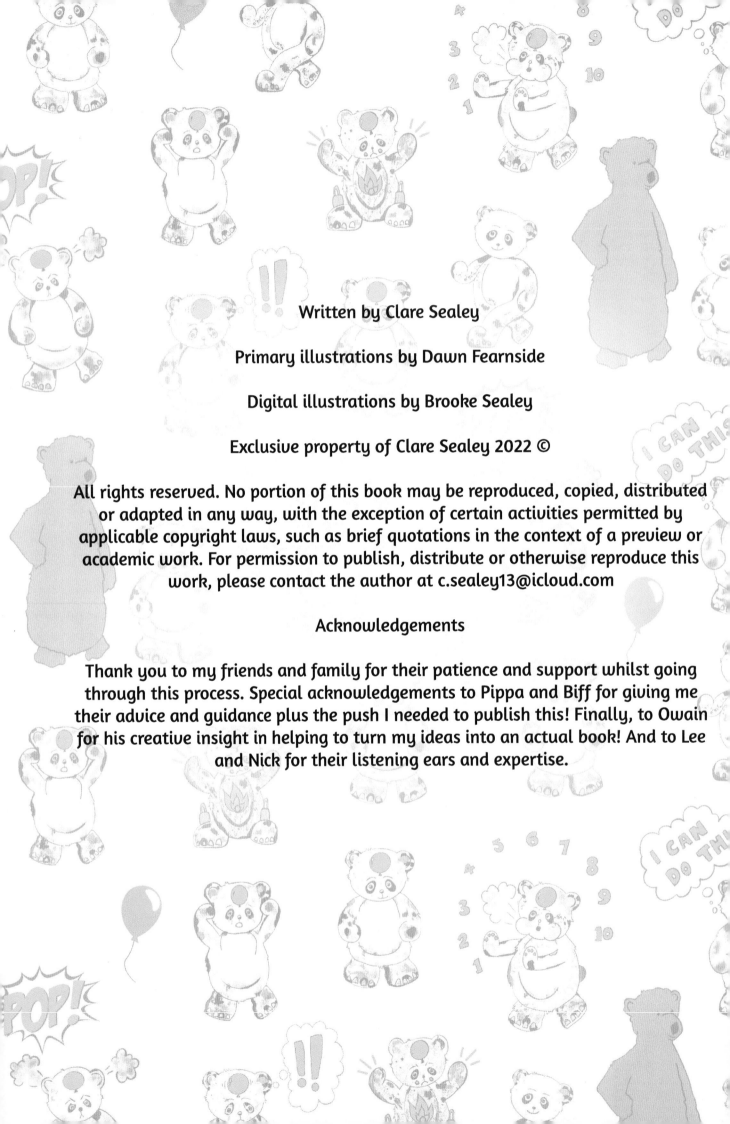

Written by Clare Sealey

Primary illustrations by Dawn Fearnside

Digital illustrations by Brooke Sealey

Acknowledgements

Thank you to my friends and family for their patience and support whilst going through this process. Special acknowledgements to Pippa and Biff for giving me their advice and guidance plus the push I needed to publish this! Finally, to Owain for his creative insight in helping to turn my ideas into an actual book! And to Lee and Nick for their listening ears and expertise.

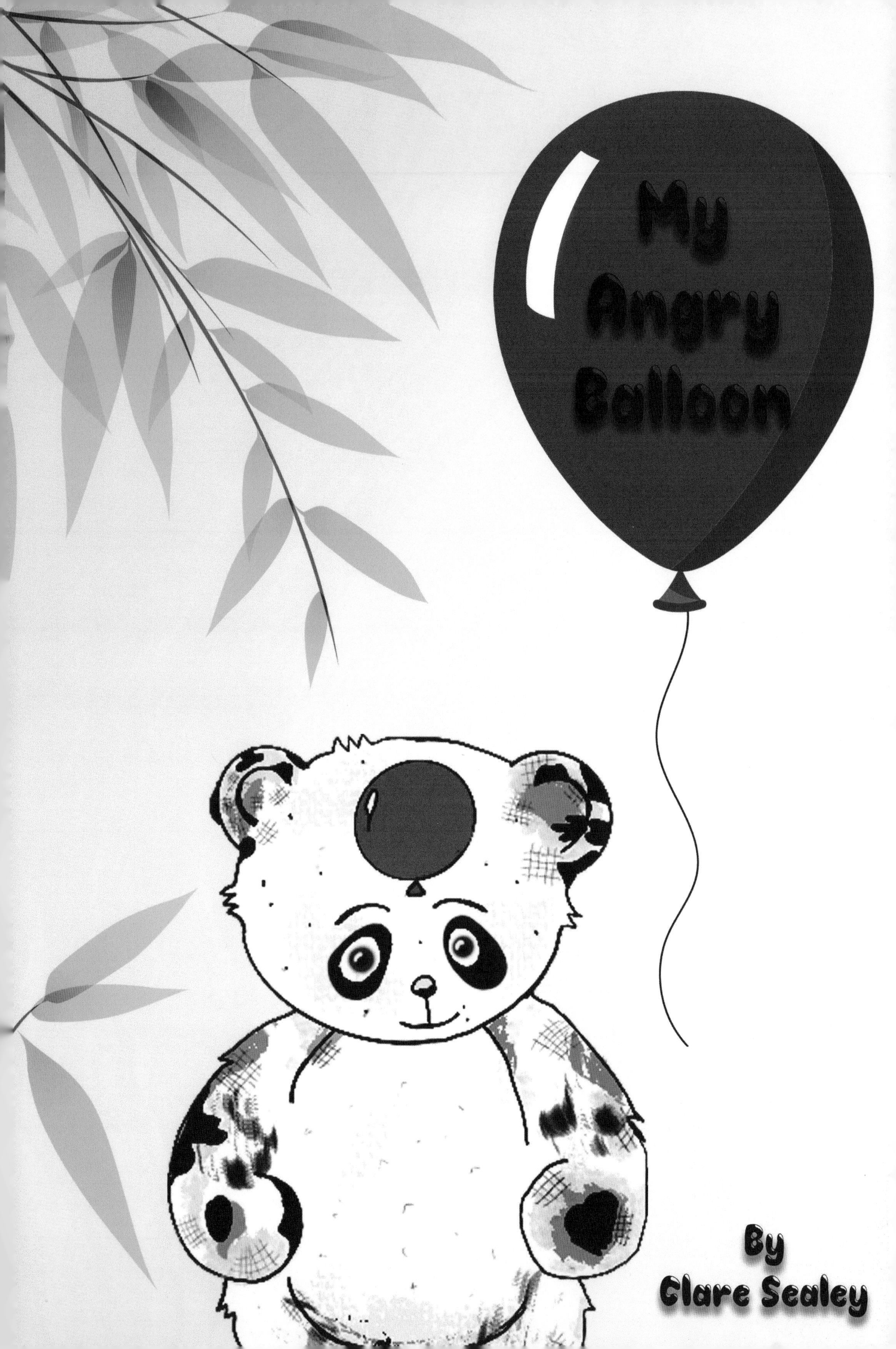
My Angry Balloon
By Clare Sealey

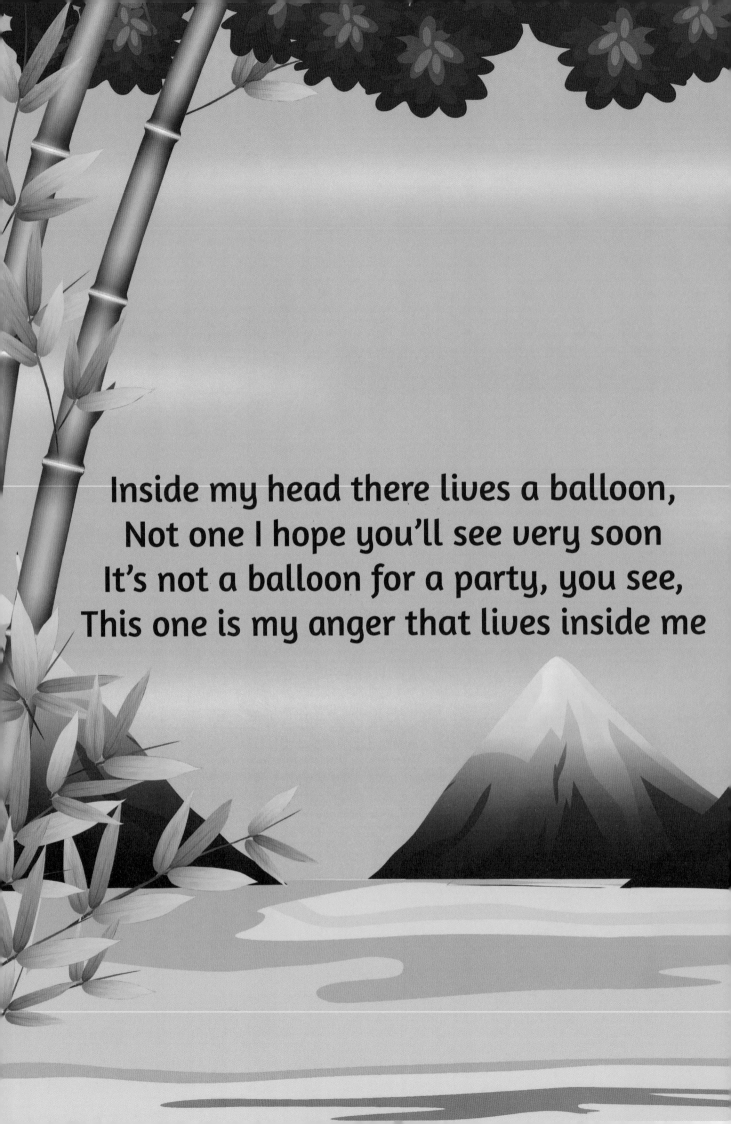

Inside my head there lives a balloon,
Not one I hope you'll see very soon
It's not a balloon for a party, you see,
This one is my anger that lives inside me

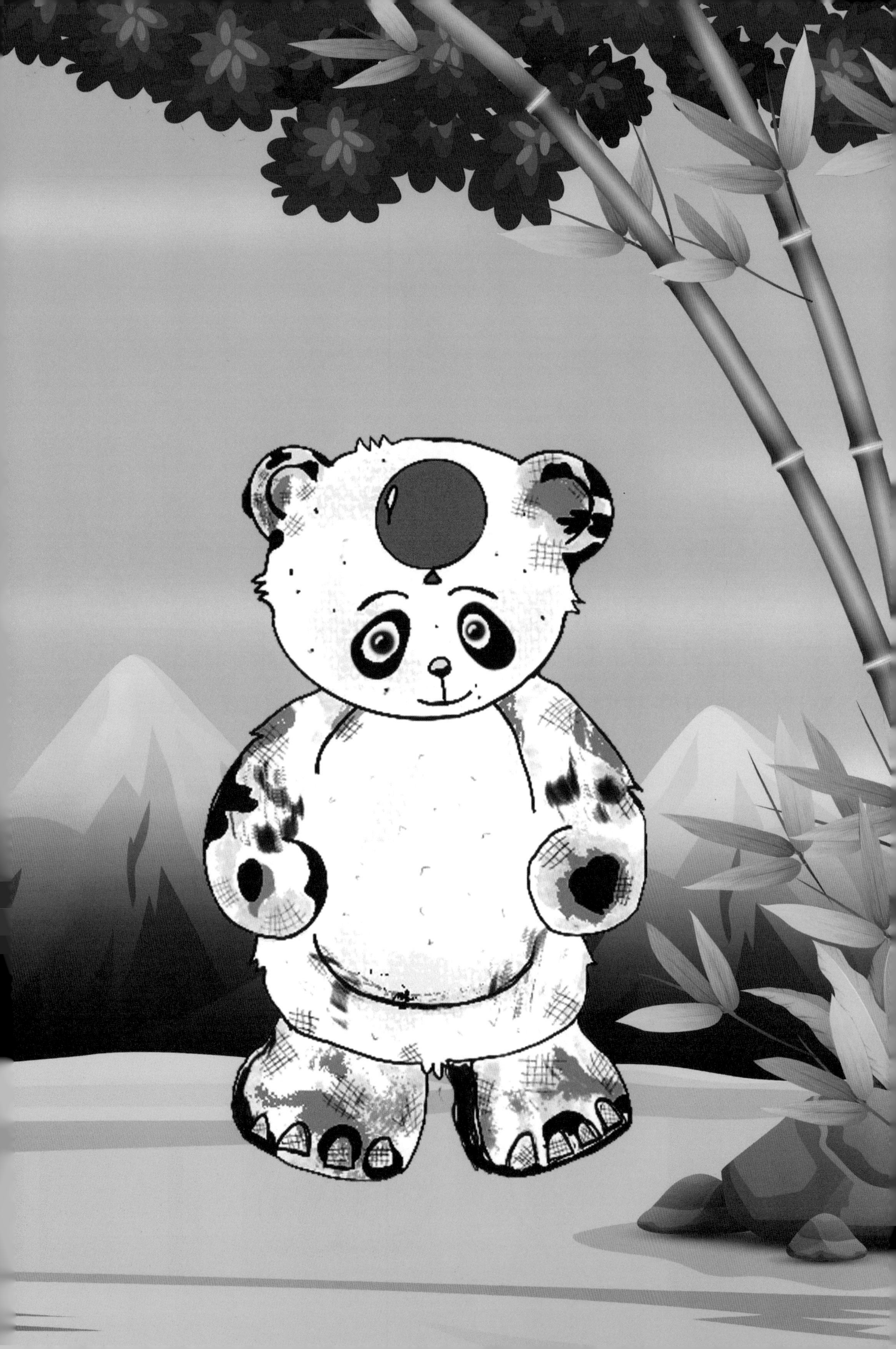

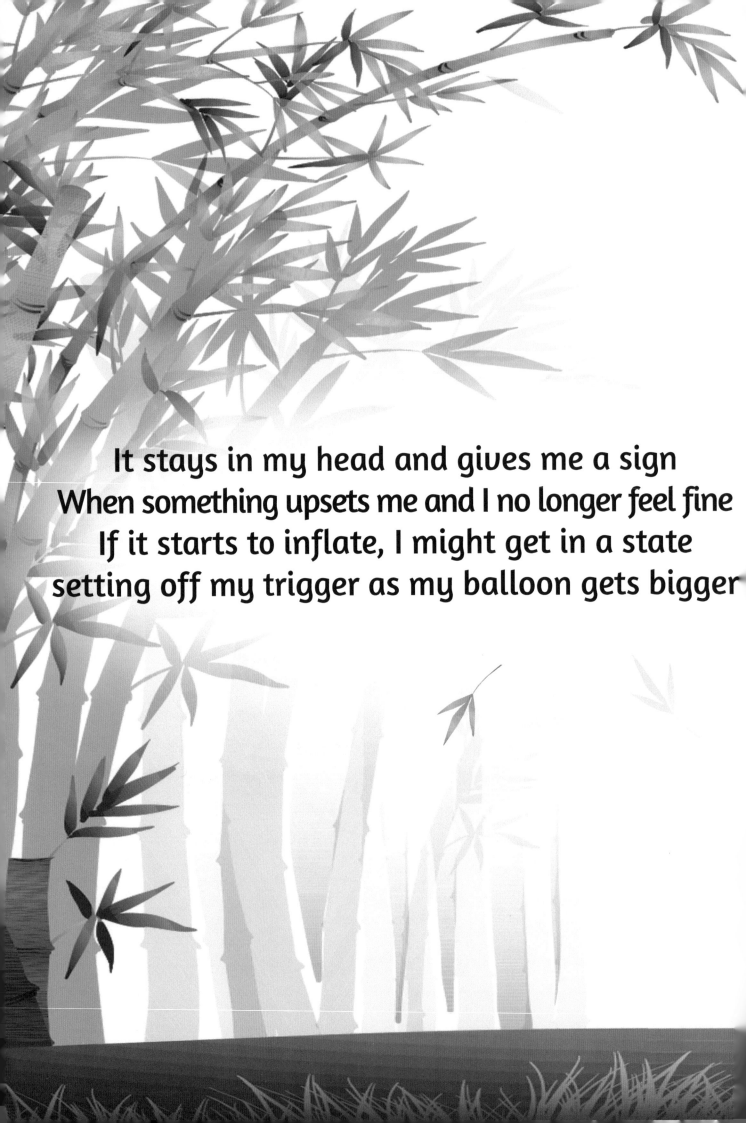

It stays in my head and gives me a sign
When something upsets me and I no longer feel fine
If it starts to inflate, I might get in a state
setting off my trigger as my balloon gets bigger

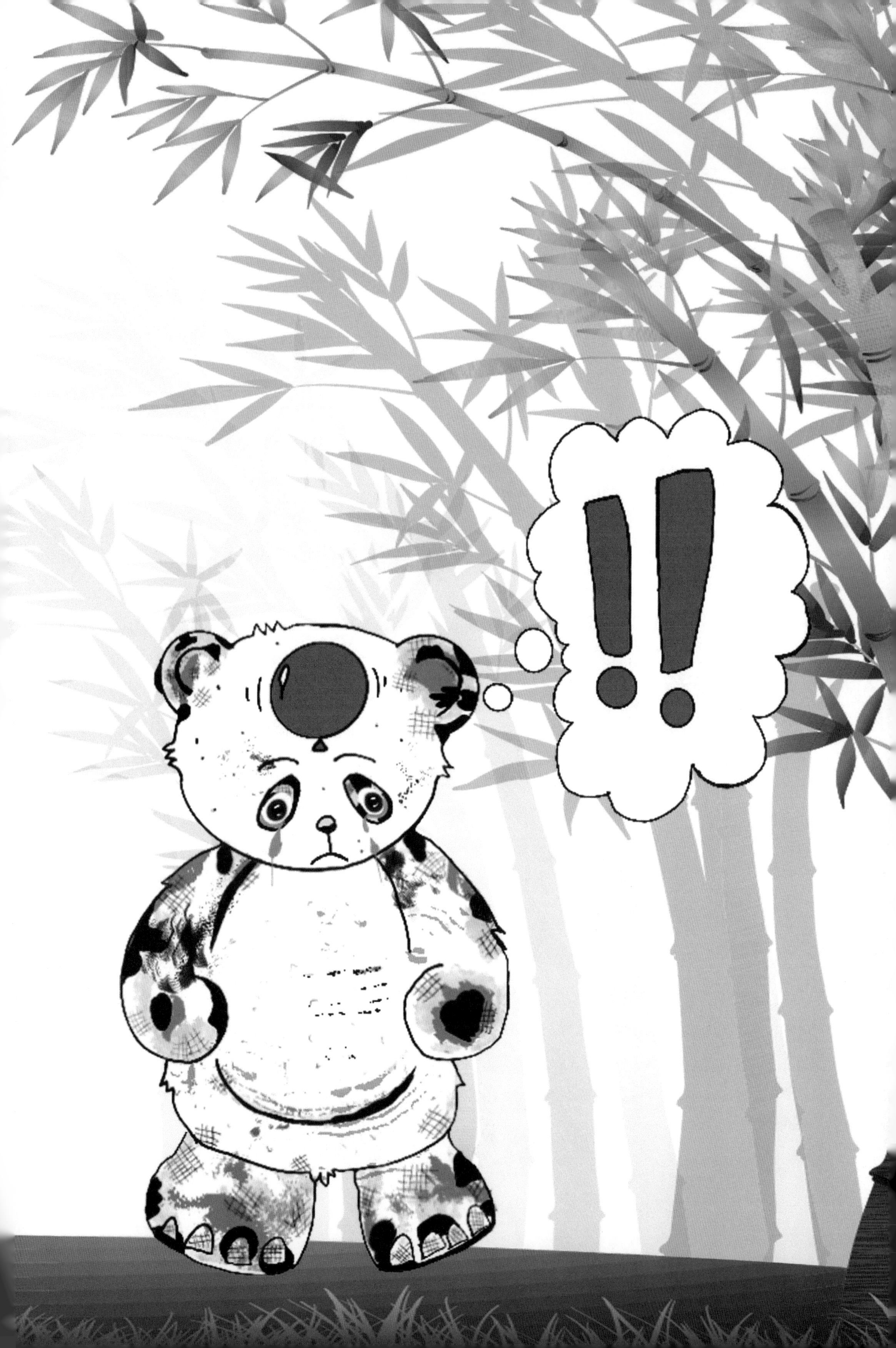
!!

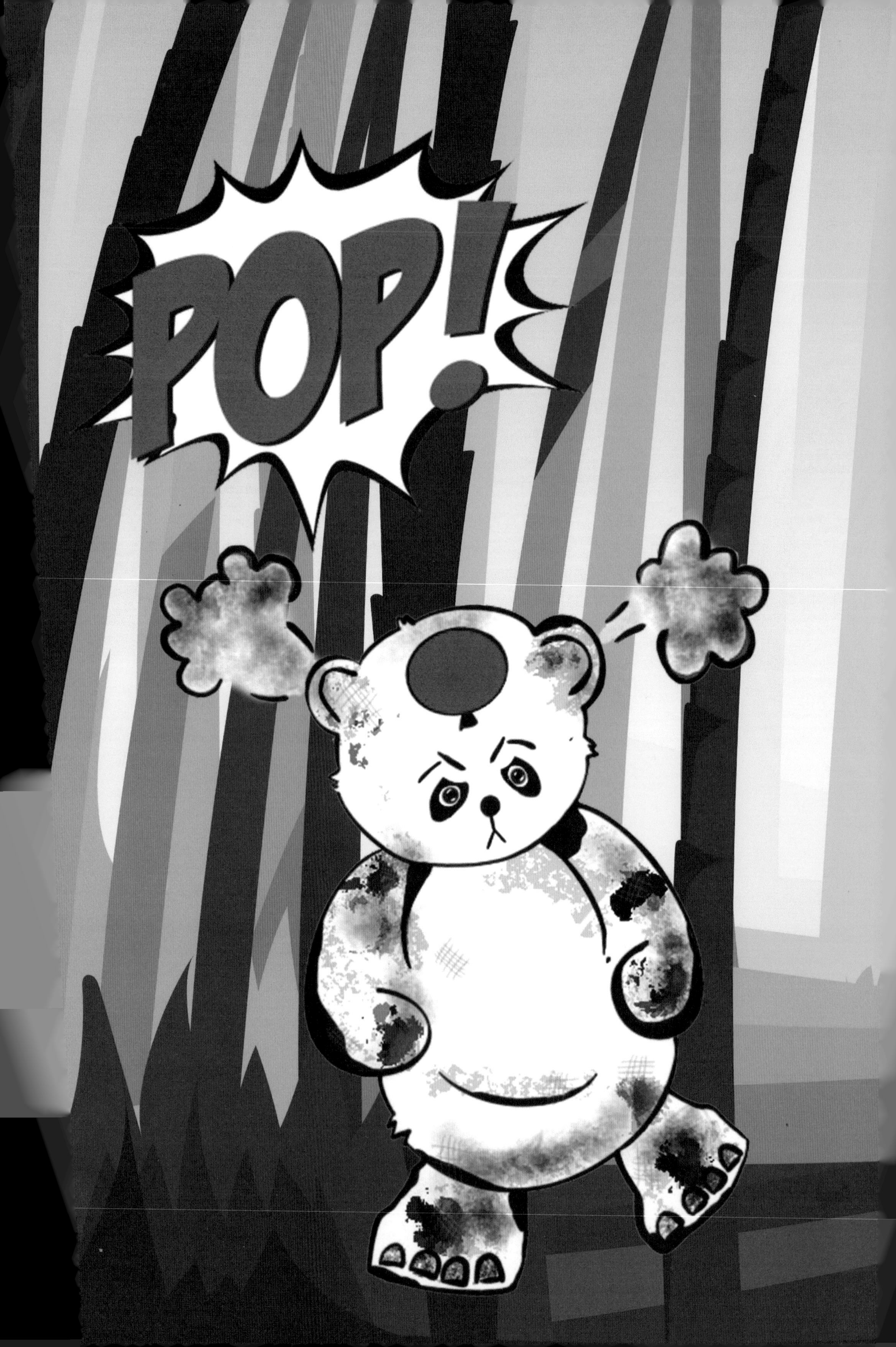
POP!

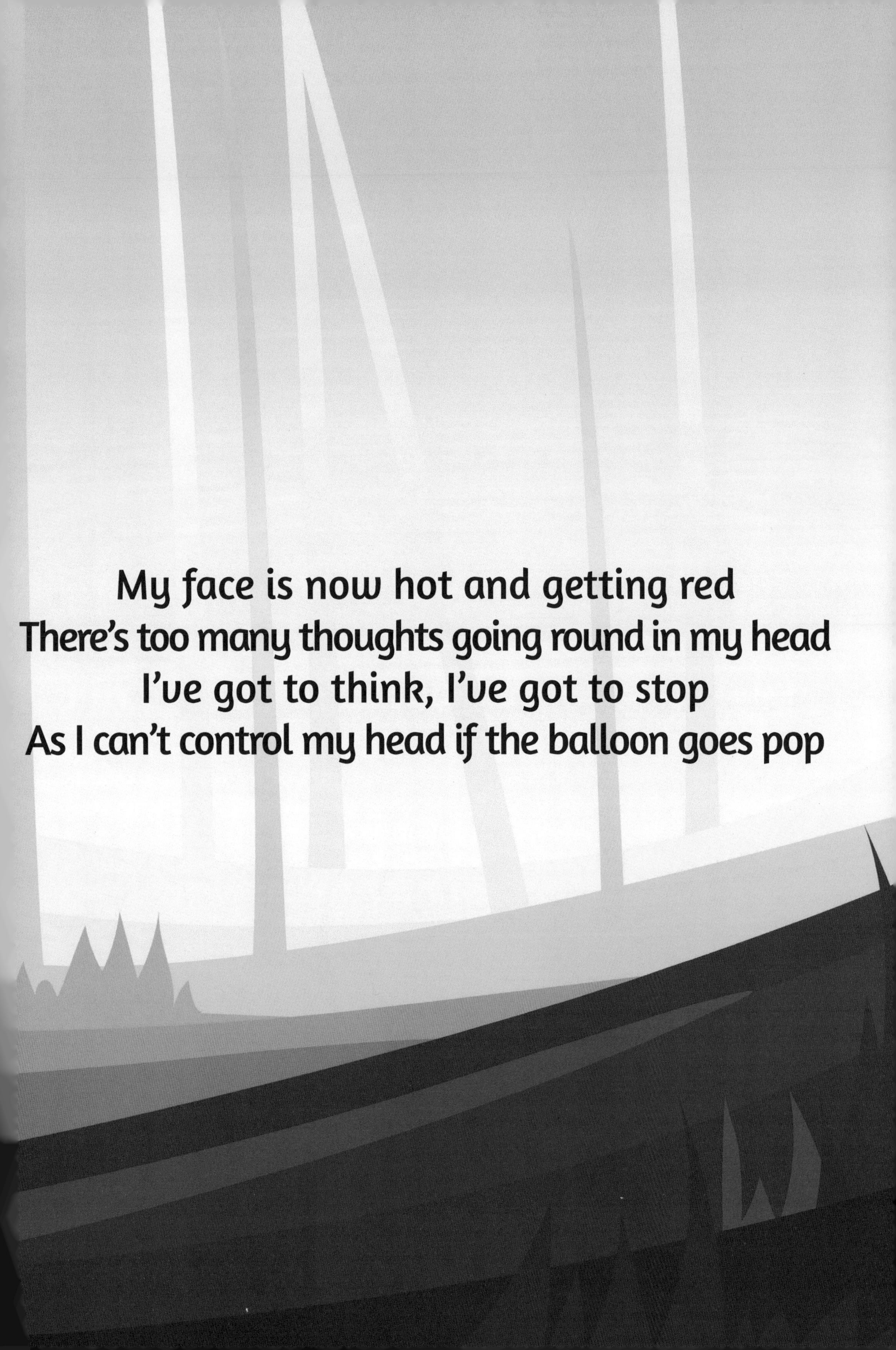

My face is now hot and getting red
There's too many thoughts going round in my head
I've got to think, I've got to stop
As I can't control my head if the balloon goes pop

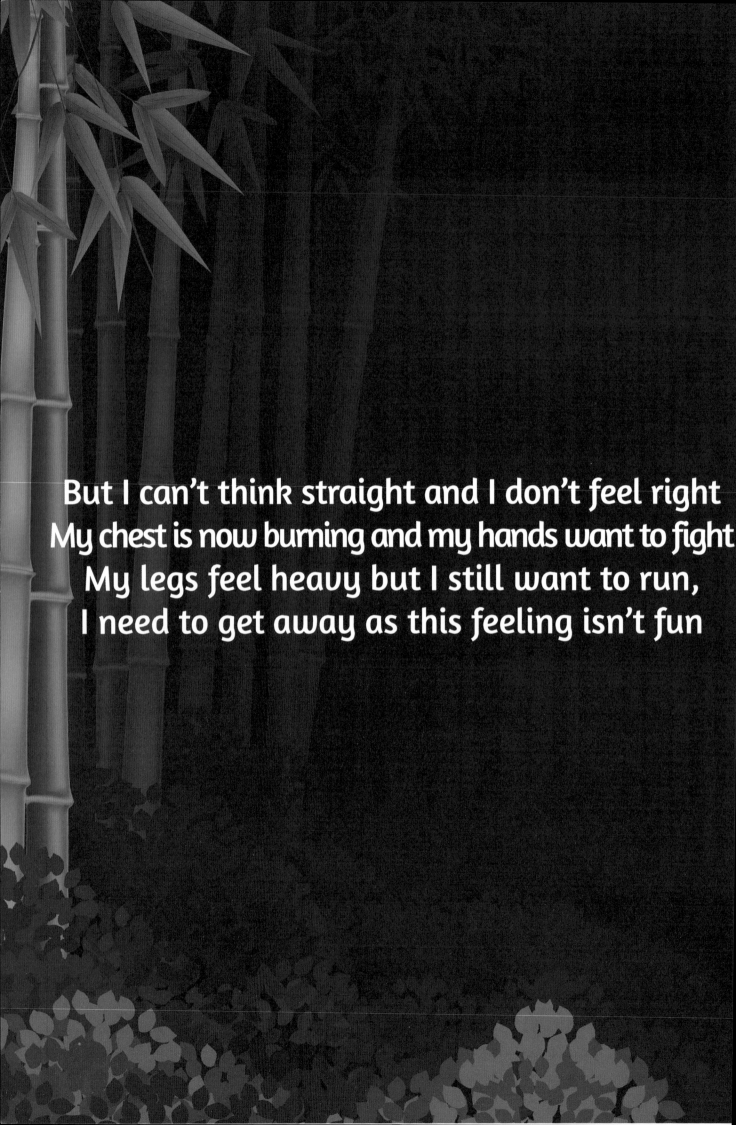

But I can't think straight and I don't feel right
My chest is now burning and my hands want to fight
My legs feel heavy but I still want to run,
I need to get away as this feeling isn't fun

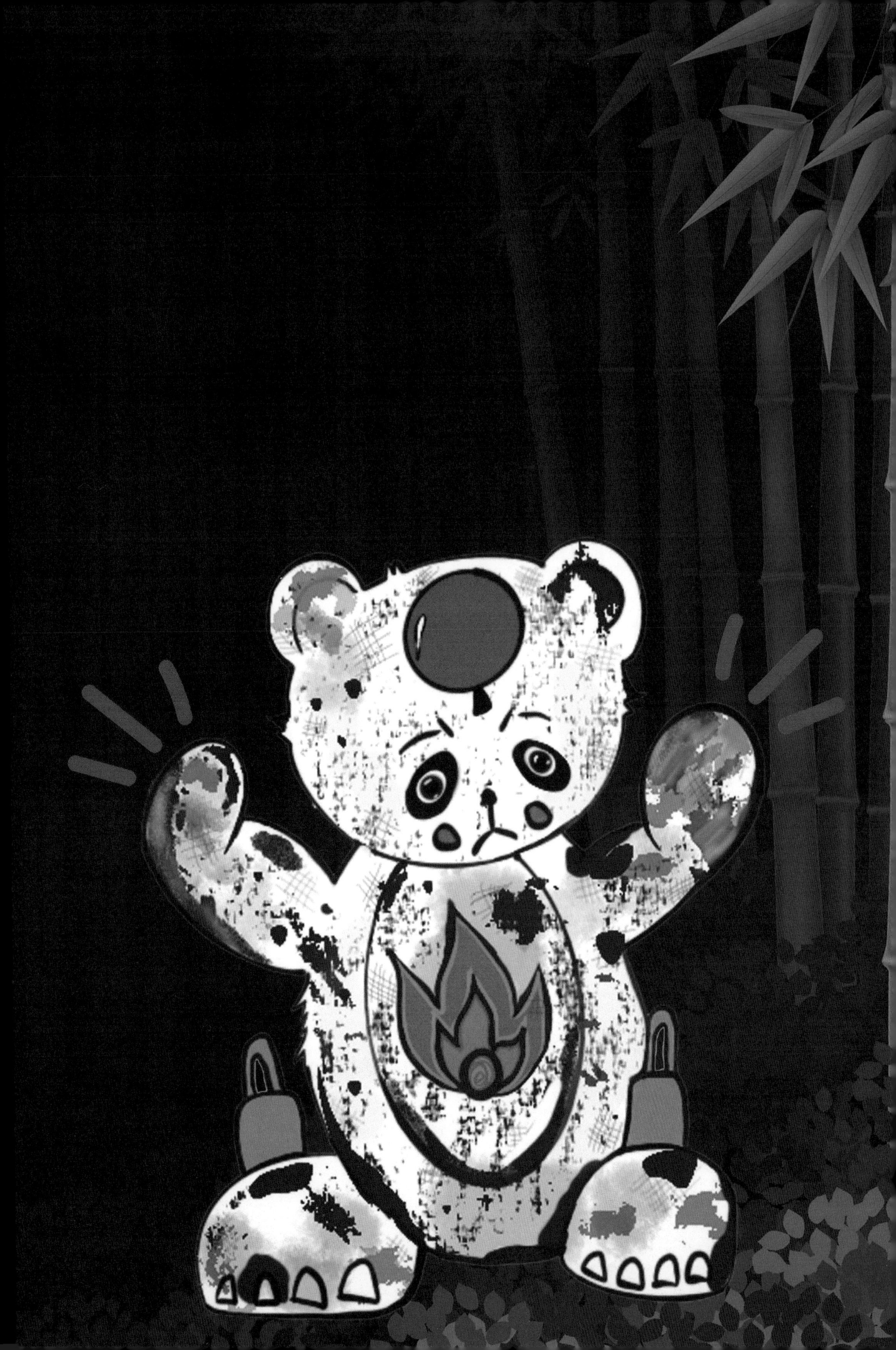

I feel in a panic, I want to cry
But others might laugh as I pass them by
My mouth feels dry, yet I still want to shout
I need something or someone to help me out

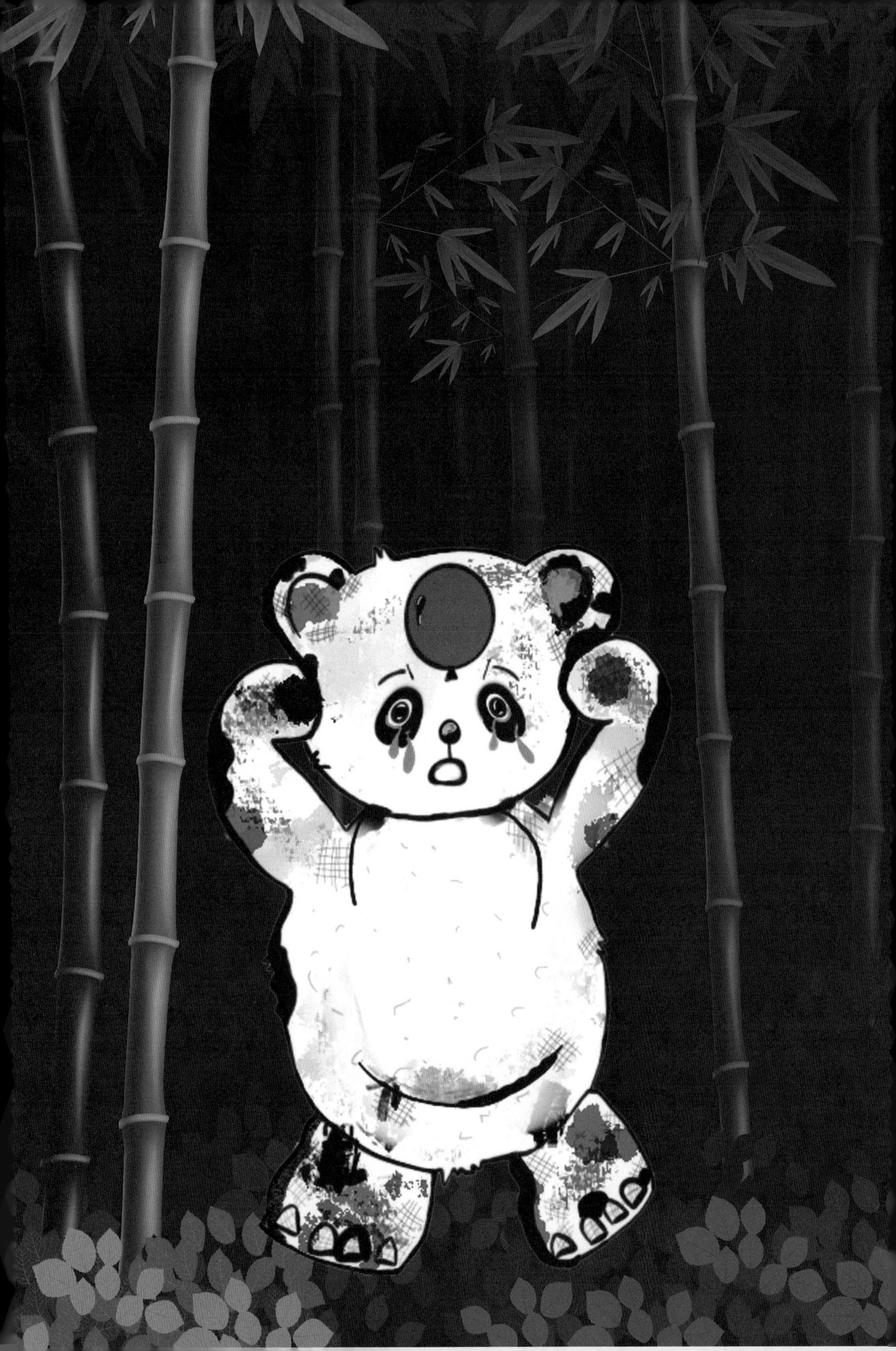

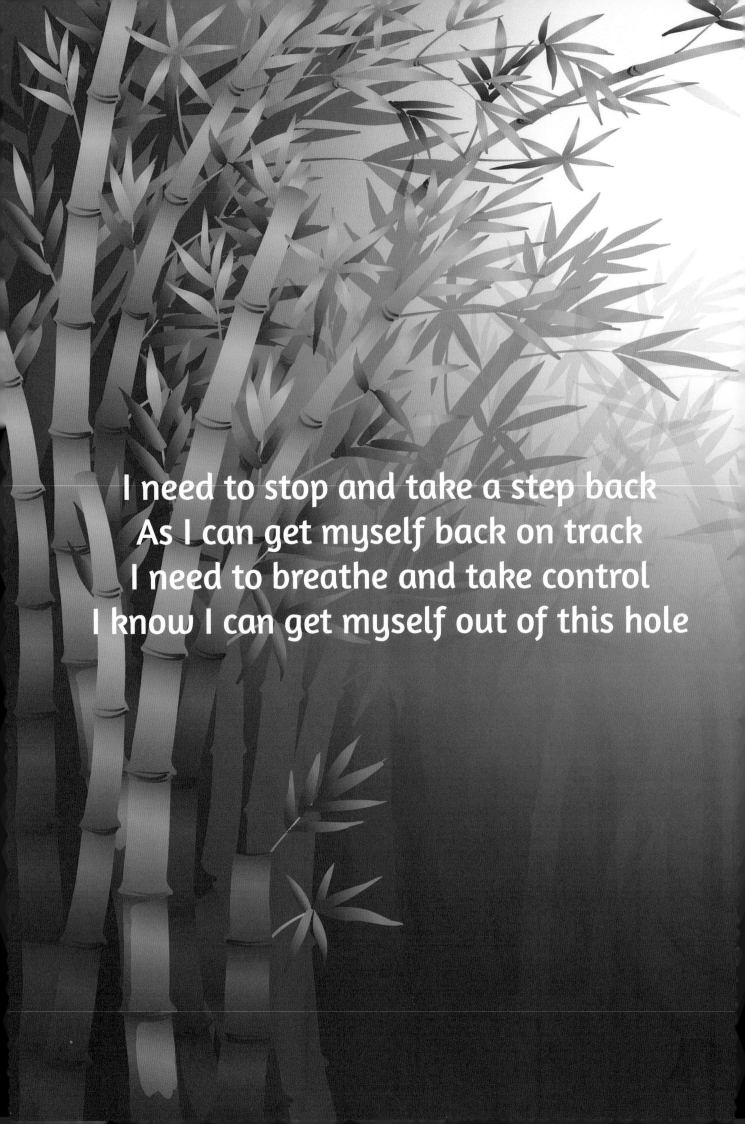

I need to stop and take a step back
As I can get myself back on track
I need to breathe and take control
I know I can get myself out of this hole

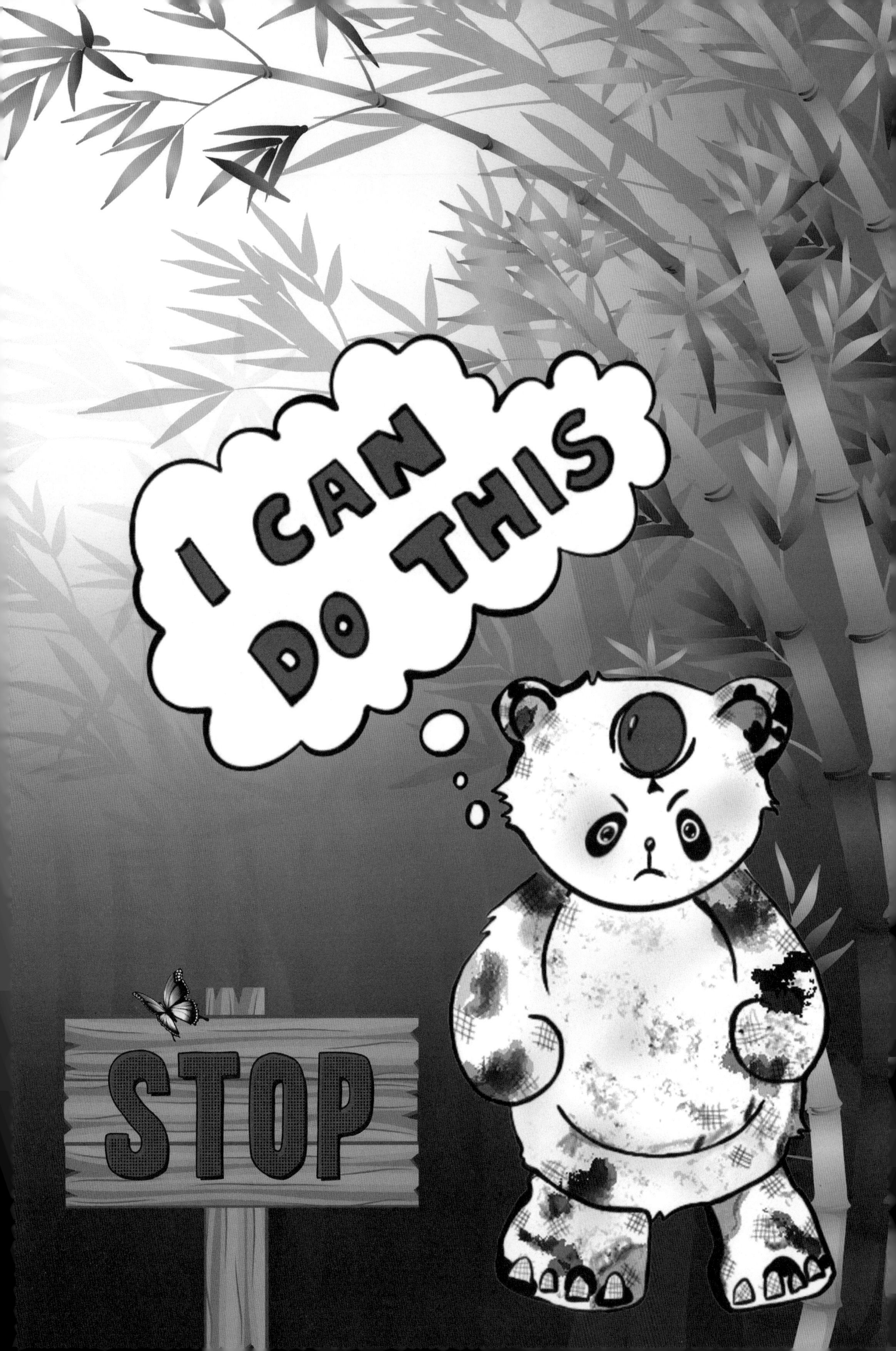
I CAN DO THIS
STOP

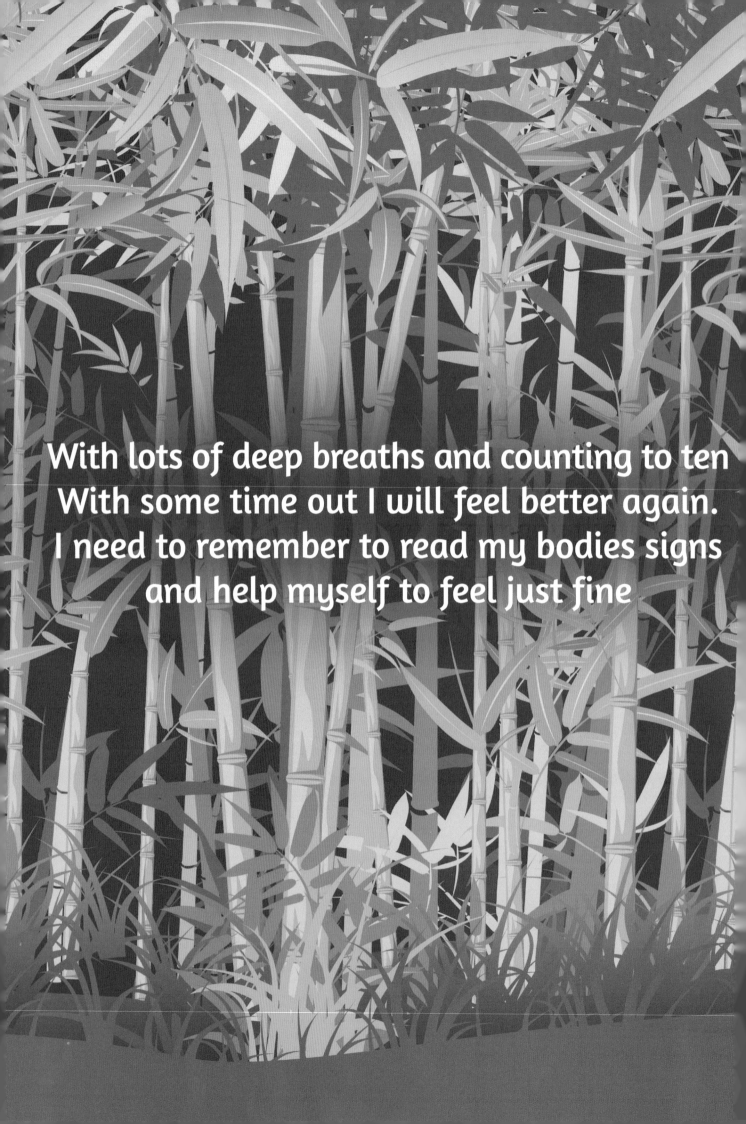

With lots of deep breaths and counting to ten
With some time out I will feel better again.
I need to remember to read my bodies signs
and help myself to feel just fine

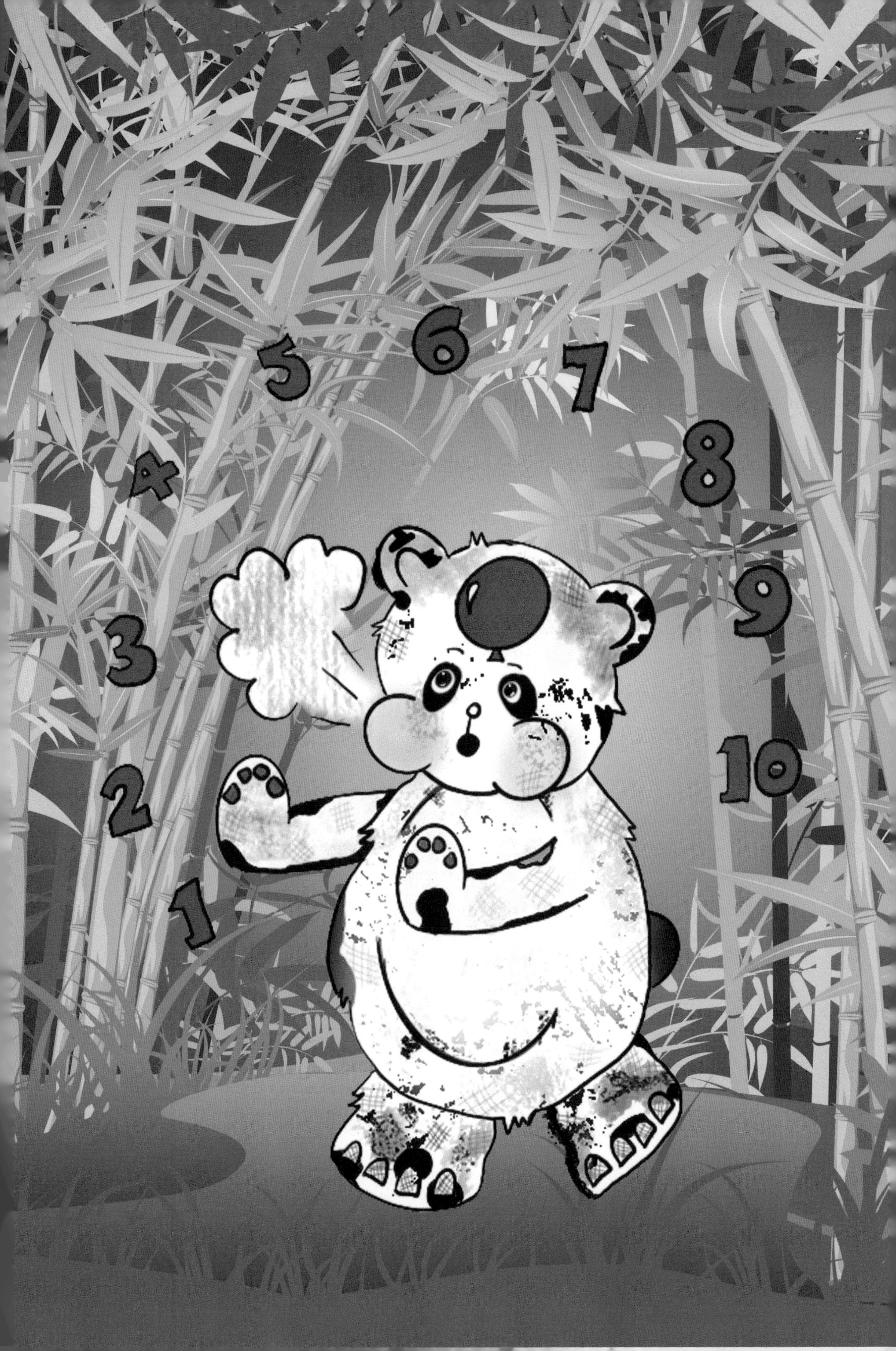
1
2
3
4
5
6
7
8
9
10

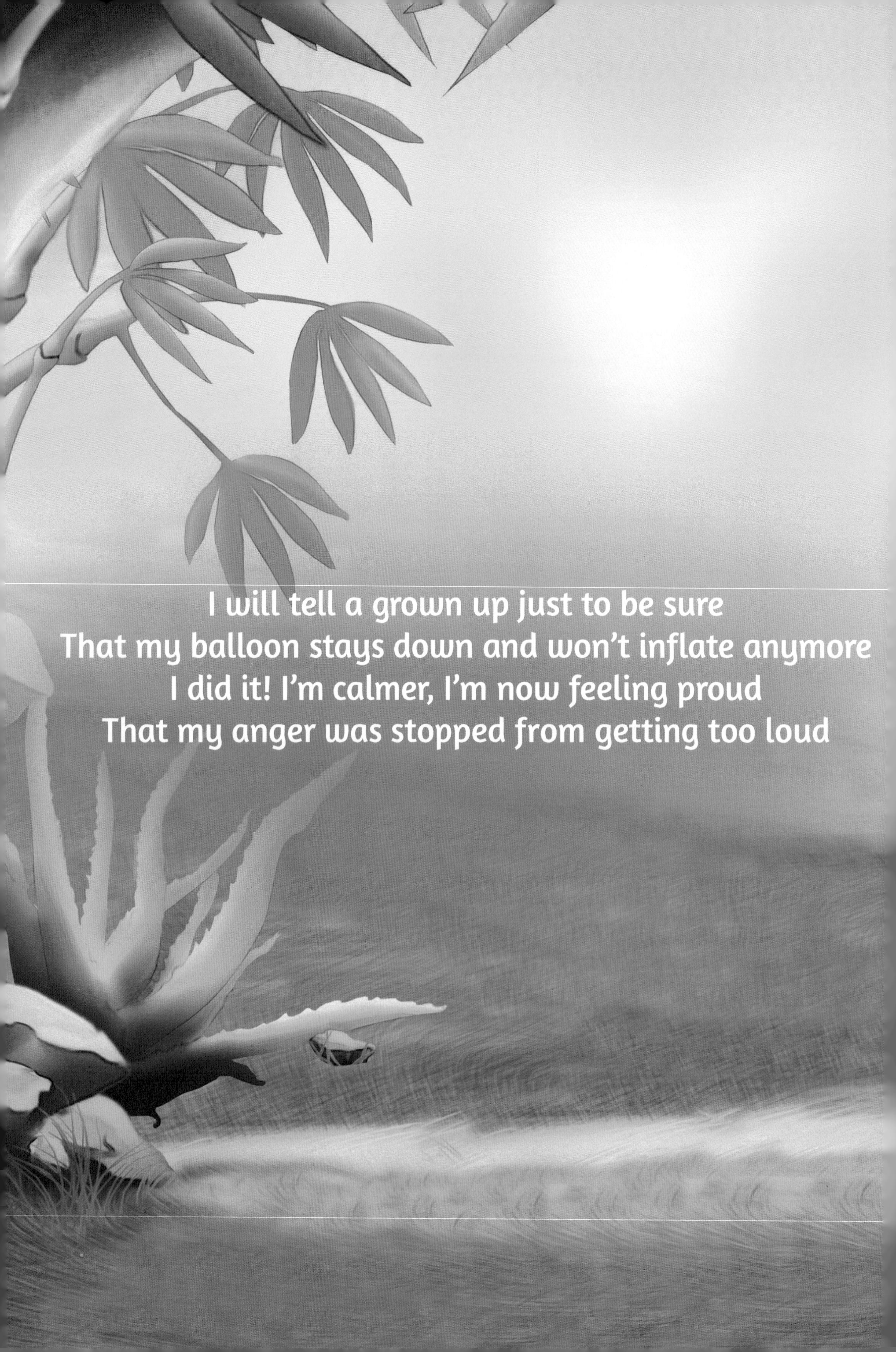

I will tell a grown up just to be sure
That my balloon stays down and won't inflate anymore
I did it! I'm calmer, I'm now feeling proud
That my anger was stopped from getting too loud

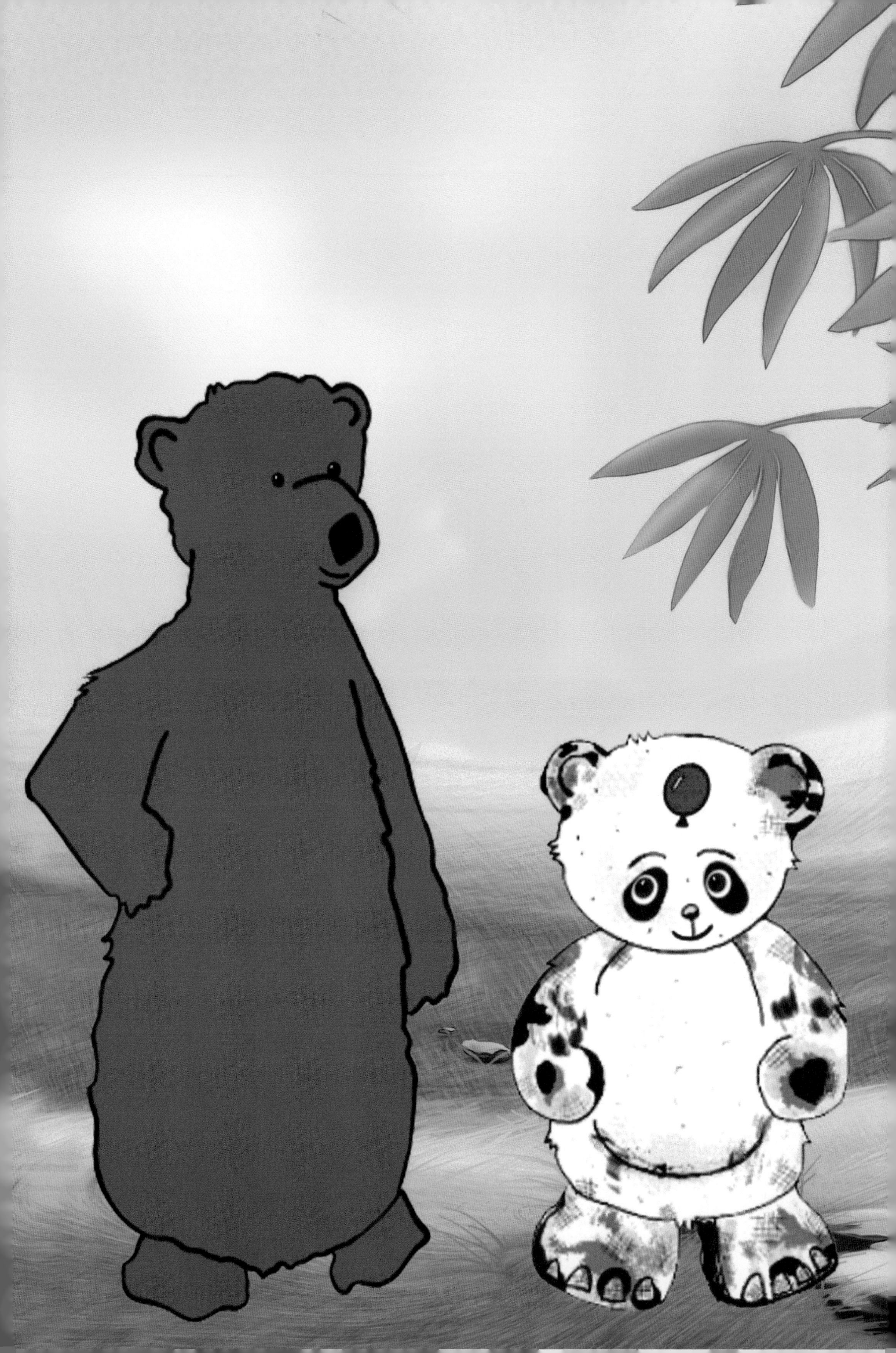

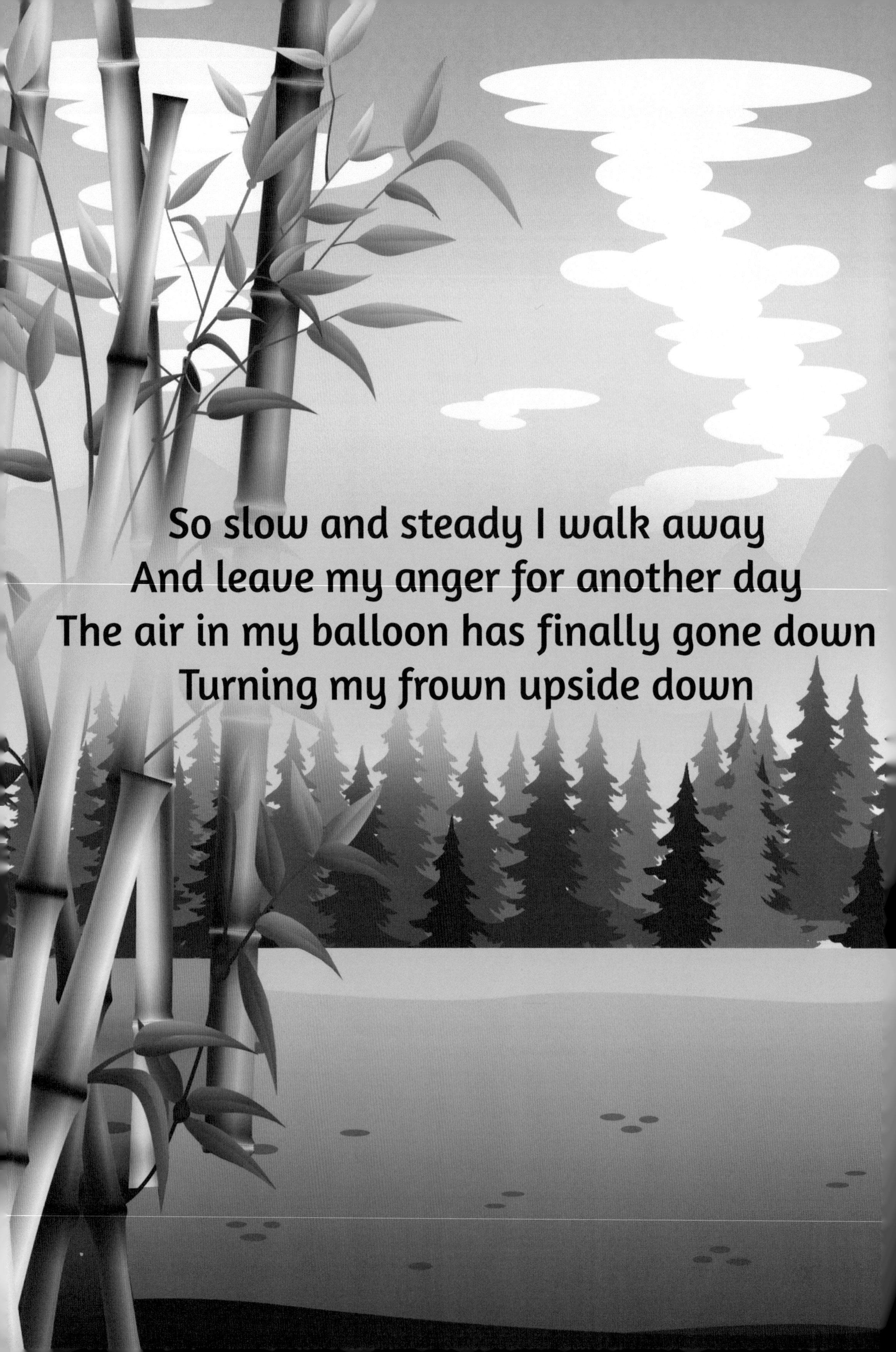

So slow and steady I walk away
And leave my anger for another day
The air in my balloon has finally gone down
Turning my frown upside down

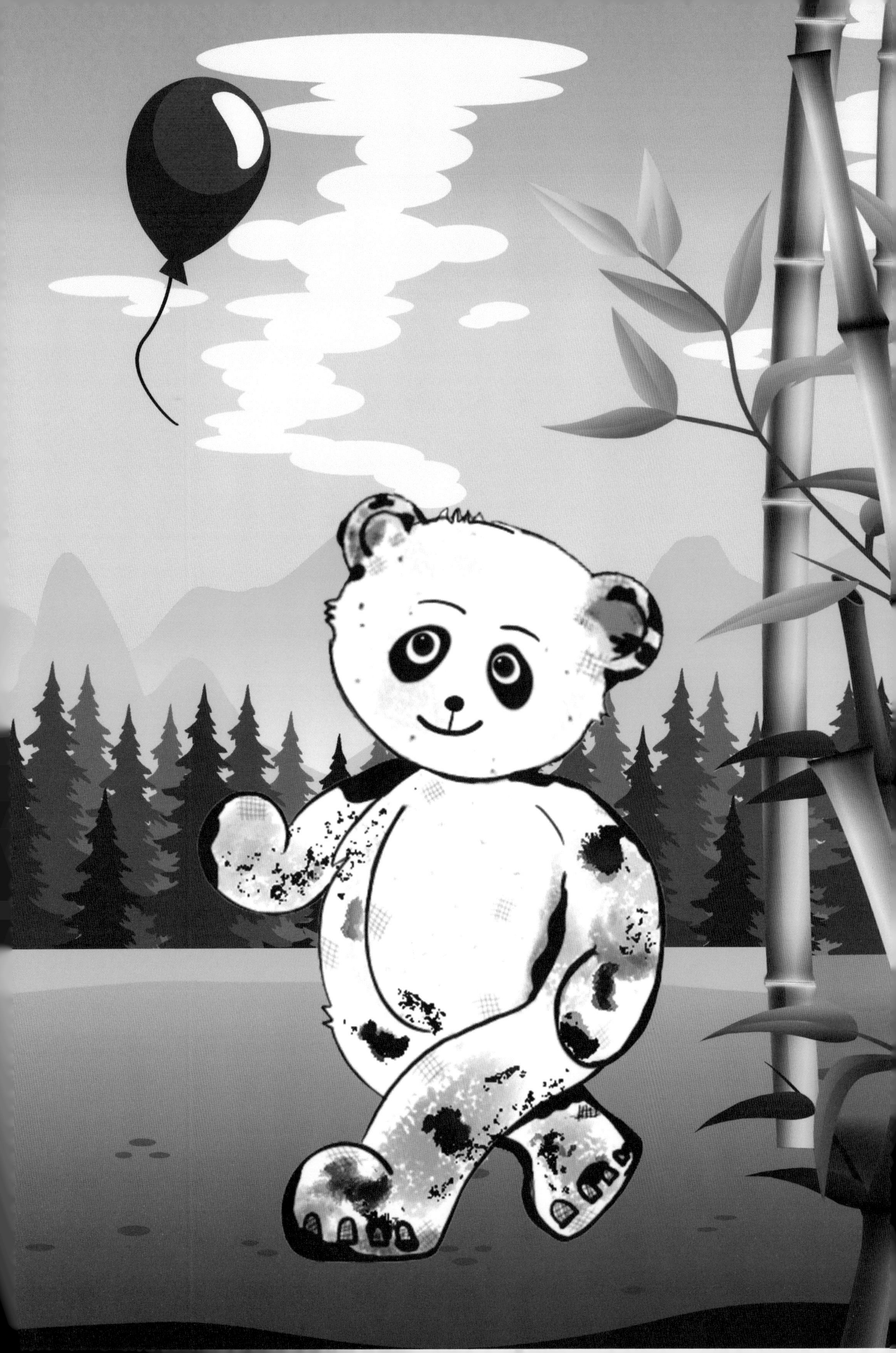

POP!
!!
I CAN DO THIS
1 2 3 4 5 6 7 8 9 10